GROUND SQUIRRELS

GROUND SQUIRRELS

Colleen Stanley Bare

Illustrated with photographs by the author

DODD, MEAD & COMPANY
New York

A SKYLIGHT BOOK

1 2 3 4 5 6 7 8 9 10

Library of Congress Cataloging in Publication Data

Bare, Colleen Stanley.
Ground squirrels.

Includes index.
SUMMARY: Describes the life cycle of the
California ground squirrel which is commonly found
in California, Nevada, Oregon, Washington, and
northern Mexico.
1. California ground squirrel—Juvenile
literature. 2. Squirrels—Juvenile literature.
[1. California ground squirrel. 2. Squirrels]
I. Title.
QL737.R68B35   599.32′32   80–13649
ISBN 0–396–07852–4

To Grant

A California ground squirrel

INTRODUCTION

Squirrels exist almost everywhere in the world. There are about 250 species divided into ground, tree, and flying squirrels. They all belong to the family Sciuridae, which means "shadow-tail."

This book is about ground squirrels.

Ground squirrels have been around, in much the same form, for about twelve million years. They are very adaptable animals and can survive in almost any climate, from the hot desert to the cold arctic. This is because they are burrowers and can escape undesirable conditions by going underground.

They have large families and, in nature, serve as an important link in the food chain so that other animals may live. In agricultural areas, ground squirrels often come into conflict with man when they feed on his crops and cause soil erosion with their digging.

All squirrels are rodents, which are the most numerous of all mammals, characterized by four unique front teeth especially built for gnawing.

Gray-whitish shoulder bar

Coarse, brown-whitish mottled coat

Fluffy, banded tail

Pointed ears

White eye ring

Stiff, brown wh

Cheek pouches

Mouth—with 2

Front foot—4 t

Hind foot—5 t

Ground Squirrel Anatomy

There are over forty species of ground squirrels living in North America, many found in the western and central United States. They all have similar characteristics, such as cheek pouches, short ears, and furry tails. Other traits include winter hibernation, daylight activity, the digging of underground burrows, and a diet of vegetation and insects.

The species described in this book is the California, or Beechey, ground squirrel (*Citellus beecheyi*). This animal lives in the western states of California, Nevada, Oregon,

8

Washington, and in Northern Mexico. It is very common in open and semiopen country at altitudes of from sea level to over 8,000 feet.

California ground squirrels may vary in size and in their habits of hibernation, depending upon where they live and the climate of their environment.

Also mentioned in the book is another species of ground squirrel, the golden-mantled (*Citellus lateralis*), and a

A golden-mantled ground squirrel

A western gray squirrel

species of tree squirrel, the Western gray squirrel (*Sciurus griseus*).

This story is set in an ideal kind of area where ground squirrels are frequently found—in an open forest, containing fallen logs and many rocks along a river, with dry, loose soil suitable for digging. Here they can dig their burrows, feed on their chosen menu of nuts and seeds, and lead peaceful lives away from man.

One sunny afternoon early in March, when the forest was still dressed in its winter clothes, a hungry coyote prowled among the trees. He was hunting a meal.

Most of the living things were not out yet, for the air was chilly and the snow was just melting. It would be several weeks before spring would arrive, greening the trees and the plants which would provide food for the animals.

The coyote sniffed and pawed at the ground, looking for squirrel burrows. He hoped to find a ground squirrel for supper. They often came out in March to begin their mating.

Meanwhile, in an underground house, a male ground squirrel awakened from his winter sleep. During the cold months he had hibernated, with his heartbeat and his breathing rate slowed down so that his body didn't need any food for awhile. Occasionally he had roused to feed on the nuts and seeds that he had gathered and stored the

Ground squirrels inhabit forests like this.

previous fall. Now, his food supply was almost gone. Like the coyote, he too was hungry, and he started to leave the burrow to look for food. During storms, the winds had blown leaves and dirt into the entrance of his den, and he had to dig his way out.

As he popped out of the burrow hole, he was wary. He crouched, remaining absolutely still. The only parts of him that moved were his sides, when he breathed, and his eyes that occasionally blinked. This is called *freezing*, which squirrels usually do each time they leave their burrows, sometimes for as long as three minutes. By holding still, they are less likely to be seen by their many enemies.

When the male ground squirrel finally moved, he didn't go far. He began to search along the ground looking for nuts that might have been buried there in the fall by other squirrels. His keen sense of smell told him just where to look, and he soon found a plump acorn a few inches below the ground. He dug at the soil, removed the nut with his

Squirrels freeze when leaving their burrows, to be sure no predators are nearby.

Eating a nut

forepaws, and quickly hulled it. Stuffing the nut into his
mouth, he chewed rapidly as he watched for danger.

Then he hopped onto a log and sunned himself. He sat
high enough so that he could look out over the forest floor.

Once he saw another squirrel run across an open space among the trees, but it quickly disappeared into a burrow.

Suddenly, the male ground squirrel froze. His sensitive ears had heard frightening sounds—a sharp bark followed by a mournful howl.

It was the voice of the hungry coyote that was still some distance away and had not yet noticed the male ground squirrel.

The brownish coloring of the squirrel's coat, mixed with shades of gray, tan, and white, matched the log and the soil and the trees so well that he could hardly be seen. He blended perfectly with the background of the forest. Still sitting on the log, he remained frozen.

Coyotes are among the squirrel's most feared enemies,

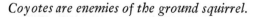

Coyotes are enemies of the ground squirrel.

for they are very crafty hunters. Sometimes they even go squirrel hunting in pairs. One coyote attracts the attention of the squirrel while the other one sneaks up and grabs the small animal from behind.

The male ground squirrel stayed frozen until he heard a crackly, rustling sound like pawsteps on dried leaves. He gave a loud chirp and leaped from the log, bounding across the ground. His long bushy tail stretched straight out behind him as he raced toward the safety of his burrow.

Swiftly, the coyote chased after him, but the ground squirrel kept ahead. He dived into the mouth of his underground house and disappeared.

The coyote, which resembled a large dog, pawed at the entrance of the burrow with its front feet. The squirrel den was an old one, with long winding tunnels dug deep into the ground. The coyote soon gave up and turned away to hunt for some other animal, perhaps a gopher or a mouse, for his dinner.

Later, the male ground squirrel came back out of his

A squirrel runs rapidly to the safety of its burrow.

burrow. He paused at the mouth of his den and froze. Soon his nose began to quiver as he sniffed the air. He was still hungry, and he could smell the sweet odors of fresh seeds just beginning to sprout in the soil. He lowered his head and began to forage for food.

When squirrels *forage* they walk along with their noses to the ground, scratching at the dirt with their forefeet. Their smelling sense leads them to plants, grasses, roots, bulbs, and leaves. Other favorite foods are berries, fruits, mushrooms, and grain. Sometimes they eat small insects, birds, and eggs. But the best ground squirrel foods of all are the acorns, nuts, and seeds which they can store away in their dens.

It was a warm day for March, and the male ground squirrel soon found a number of other squirrels also out foraging. They had just awakened and wanted to eat. Usually he got along very well with his squirrel neighbors, most of whom lived in nearby dens. They often fed side by side without any trouble. Now, however, it was the mating season, which was also the fighting season.

The male ground squirrel had begun to feed on some

Squirrel foraging for food.

Nose touching is a means of communication.

buried pine nuts when he noticed a female squirrel foraging near him. He touched noses with her, which is a way
that squirrels communicate with each other. They began
to forage together.

Another male squirrel, sitting a short distance away
eating a nut, became alert. He had been in fights with
other squirrels and had scars on his face and one ear miss-

Opposite: *This squirrel has a scar on his nose and is missing an ear.*

ing. Squirrels have different personalities just like people, and this one was excitable. He quickly ran over to the male ground squirrel, stood next to him, and touched noses. Then he shoved against him and jumped at him. The two rolled on the ground and became a blur of bushy tails and brown and tan fur. They clawed and scratched at each other, biting with their sharp teeth and chattering. Finally, the squirrel with the scarred face ran away.

The male ground squirrel licked at the cuts and scratches he had received during the fight. Then he rolled over and rubbed himself in the loose soil, giving himself a dust bath. He was lucky. Sometimes squirrels are seriously injured or even killed during their fights. He got up, shook himself, and went to look for the female that had run off when the fight began.

He found her sitting on a large rock, sunning herself, but she was not alone. Another larger, darker male had just approached her and touched noses with her.

The smaller male ground squirrel walked stiffly toward the other male, with his tail arched and his fur raised. Not easily bluffed, the larger male began to circle the smaller

Two squirrels sunning themselves—a favorite pastime.

one and pushed against him. They hit and bit at each other's head and neck until, suddenly, the larger squirrel turned and began to run. The smaller male ground squirrel took off after him in a chase until the intruder disappeared into a burrow.

Ready for a fight . . .

. . . circling . . .

...shoving...

...fighting ferociously...

...the chase.

Later the male ground squirrel mated with the female, and they spent time together in her burrow.

The male squirrel soon left his mate and moved into another den. This was a simple burrow, small and shallow, located some distance away from the female ground squirrel. He lived in the den alone.

Meanwhile, the female ground squirrel had become very busy. Her babies would be born in about four weeks, and she too found herself a new home.

She moved into an old, empty burrow that had been used by many squirrels before her. Its opening was partially hidden by a clump of brush which would make it safer from predators. She first had to clean out the entrance to the burrow to get inside. Using her front feet, she scooped out the dead leaves and earth with her flattened paws. Then she kicked out the loosened soil with her hind feet. She only dug for about a minute at a time when she stopped and froze. She was always wary, alert to danger.

Squirrels often have burrows which are hidden by bushes.

Once inside, the female ground squirrel chose a location at the back of the burrow in a separate little chamber. This is where she would build her nest and prepare for the arrival of her babies.

While this was going on, the male ground squirrel was spending his time sleeping in his den, sitting on a large rock in the sun on warm days, and foraging. He also scratched a lot. Using his hind foot, he scratched at his face, ears, neck, and sides. Like all squirrels, he seemed to itch all over. This is because they have fleas, lice, ticks, mites, and other parasites that bite them.

The male ground squirrel no longer paid any attention to the female. He was completely unaware of the preparations she was making for the birth of the babies.

The female ground squirrel started to gather materials for her nest, but a storm interfered. Whistling winds and heavy rains kept her waiting, cozily, three feet underground in her burrow. Squirrels don't like to be cold or wet.

When the rains stopped, the female left her burrow and began her collecting. She dug up dry grasses and plants

Because of fleas, squirrels scratch a lot.

and stuffed them into her mouth, making many trips back
and forth to carry them to the nest chamber. Often she
had to tug on tall stems to pull them loose from the

ground. Extra long stalks were folded many times with her forefeet, like an accordion, until they would fit into her mouth crosswise. She was careful never to choose green leaves or wet grasses that might decay in the nest. She took only the dried materials such as leaves, roots, plant stems, dry grass blades, and stalks.

Sometimes she was joined by one or two other squirrels, also gathering materials for their nests. Then there was a hustle bustle, and flurry of squirrel activity.

Using the dry matter that she had collected, the female ground squirrel built her nest in the burrow. Its firm outer wall was made of the heavier, coarse vegetation like twigs and thick stalks. The inside became a soft bed of fine grasses and leaves. The nest was oval-shaped like an egg and was about ten inches around and eight inches tall. It was small because the babies would be small—only about the size of a human thumb. Now the underground nursery was ready.

One night seven tiny squirrels were born. This was an

Collecting grasses for her nest

average number, although there could have been as many as twelve. They were hairless, toothless, blind, and they could not hear.

For six weeks the mother and her young remained in the nest. Being a mammal, she was able to feed them with warm milk from her body. They snuggled against her, suckling and sleeping. Their eyes did not open for three to four weeks, and by then their bodies were covered with a soft grayish tan fur. The mother squirrel sometimes left the nest to forage for food for herself. But she never went far nor stayed away for long, and she always watched for her enemies. The helpless babies in the burrow could not stay alive without her.

As the babies grew older and stronger, they started to move about. After they could see and hear, they nuzzled and wrestled each other and roamed the burrow. Baby squirrels are curious, and they often wandered into the main tunnel of the den, getting closer to the outside entrance. One of the litter was especially bold and lively. He

Baby ground squirrels look the same as adults.

often poked and shoved at the others and nibbled at them with his sharp new teeth. He also ran farther down the tunnel than anyone else.

The mother squirrel did not object to her babies' wander-

Some squirrels are especially lively and curious.

A blue jay

ings. They were growing very fast and soon would be able to leave the nest.

One morning she left the burrow to forage and to drink from the river close by. It was late May, and spring had cast its magic spell over the forest. The budding trees were now fully dressed in leaf green. Plants were blooming, and the tender green grasses tasted sweet to the mother squirrel. She hunted for grasshoppers and crickets, and she found a beetle to add to her meal. The fresh smells of the forest in springtime lured her farther and farther away from the nest burrow.

Suddenly she froze.

A blue jay screamed its shrill call of alarm. Then she

The bald eagle is a predator of the ground squirrel.

heard the weak chirp of a frightened young squirrel. She galloped back to the burrow, but it was too late.

The lively young squirrel had led his brothers and sisters through the dark tunnel into the outside world. They had not stopped to look and listen for predators. It was all too new and exciting. As the seven squirrels tumbled out of the den's entrance, a large eagle dived down from the trees and grabbed one of the babies by the neck. Rising swiftly, he flew away carrying the squirrel in his mouth.

The mother ground squirrel loudly chirped and chattered at the babies. They all scuttled back into the burrow.

The next morning, while the mother squirrel was out foraging, the young squirrel again led the remaining five babies back through the dark tunnel to the entrance. This time they were careful. They froze for several minutes just outside the burrow before they began to scatter. Even then they didn't wander far—except for the lively young squirrel.

He scampered across the ground, looking and listening, sniffing and pawing, smelling the good smells of the spring air. He poked his nose into several holes as he darted through the grass. Once, when he pushed his way into a strange tunnel, he smelled an unfamiliar odor and heard a hissing sound. He quickly ran out and froze, with his fluffy tail held high over his back. He had just met one of his enemies, the rattlesnake.

The young squirrel also tried climbing a tall oak tree.

This young squirrel is resting on a tree limb and scratching.

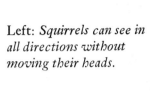
Left: *Squirrels can see in all directions without moving their heads.*

Predators of the ground squirrel include the bobcat . . .

He scurried straight up the trunk for about four feet and then, head first, ran back down again. It was such fun that he went up and down a number of times. He even sat for awhile on a limb, to rest and to scratch. Eventually, as a grown squirrel, he would be able to climb up a tree trunk fifty or sixty feet to hunt for choice acorns. But he would never swing from branch to branch, or from tree to tree, like his tree squirrel cousins.

Often he stopped to freeze, watching for predators. Like all squirrels, he had excellent vision, with his large brown eyes set high on each side of his face so that he could see practically everywhere without turning his head.

. . . and the raccoon.

So far he had met only two of his enemies, the eagle and
the rattlesnake. He didn't yet know about coyotes, hawks,
bobcats, raccoons, red foxes, badgers, weasels, skunks,
dogs, and house cats. But, even as he sat on a rock in the
warm sunshine, his instincts told him to be alert. Squirrels
spend a lot of their time sunning themselves, but they
never doze in the sun with their eyes shut. The only time
they ever relax and close their eyes to sleep is in the safety
of their underground houses.

Soon other young squirrels came out of their burrows
and began to play. The lively young squirrel joined them
and they romped and tussled. They chased each other,
waving their tails from side to side, and rolled on the

ground, kicking and biting and shoving. They seemed to fight just like adults, but they were "play fighting" and were gentle.

One squirrel, with a scar on his nose, began to circle around the lively young squirrel and poked at him with a front paw. This was a challenge to wrestle, and the young

This young squirrel has already been in a fight and has a scar on its nose.

Four razor-sharp front teeth. These can cause trouble if they don't meet.

squirrel struck back. They jumped at each other and fell to the ground, rolling over and over. In about a minute they broke apart, and the nose-scarred squirrel suddenly froze. The lively young squirrel hurried back to his brothers and sisters that were still gathered near the burrow. There he rolled in the dirt and gave himself a dust bath. Now, after his first fight, he was ready to go into the den for a long nap.

During the next few weeks the six young squirrels began to spend more time away from the den and less time with the mother squirrel. They no longer had to depend on her for their food. They now had eighteen cheek teeth set back in their jaws for grinding. And, for gnawing, they had four razor-sharp front teeth, two above and two below, called incisors. These would continue to grow throughout their lifetimes, and the squirrels would keep the incisors worn off by chewing through hard nutshells and by gnawing off twigs and other firm materials.

At the end of June the young squirrels were about two-thirds the size of the adults. They wouldn't be full grown until August when, at age four months, they would be sixteen to nineteen inches long including a six- to nine-inch tail, and weigh one to two pounds. They were losing their baby fur coats and soon would have new, thicker ones of the same brown-tan-grayish protective coloring. Adult squirrels also molt and get a new coat of fur once a year.

By July the rays of the hot summer sun filtered through the leafy trees and warmed up the forest. The once-green meadows turned brown and the grasses became dry. Now most of the adult squirrels were curled up in their underground houses, sleeping away the summer.

Ground squirrels become ill, and even die, if they are exposed to high temperatures. Although the nights in the forest are cool, squirrels are *diurnal* which means that they only go out in the daytime. So, to get away from the heat, they spend the hot months underground, sleeping—which is called *estivating*. Before this time, they become very fat so that they can exist without any food during the two or three months of their summer sleep. Young squirrels seem able to tolerate more direct sunlight and heat than the adults and do not estivate until their second year.

The mother ground squirrel had gone to sleep, away

Squirrels become fat before estivating.

from her six babies. They could take care of themselves and didn't need her any more.

The six young squirrels left the nest burrow and found, or dug, dens of their own. Several moved into a colonial burrow shared with other squirrels. It was over thirty feet long and had many tunnels and rooms, with a number of outside entrances. These openings were at the bases of trees and rocks along a river and one, so large that a squirrel could stand up in it, was in the side of the riverbank. Other entrances were hidden in grasses and under plants, with some covered by the humus on the forest floor. Each gave the squirrels protection as they warily left the burrow.

This large colonial den had been built and added to by many squirrels over a long period of time.

The lively young squirrel dug himself a house near the river, next to a large overhanging boulder. The rock would help to protect him from predators as well as from the sun in summer and the cold in winter. He dug a rather steep tunnel, down three feet under the ground, and ended up with a small, cozy den—just five feet long and four inches in diameter. Later the house would be enlarged, by him and by other squirrels.

Squirrels have burrows in a variety of hidden places. In the base of a tree . . .

. . . under humus . . .

... in a riverbank ...

... or just on flat ground.

The young squirrel often sat on top of the rock eating, sunbathing, and scratching. He had a perfect lookout post and could see all around him.

This squirrel has its burrow near a large overhanging boulder, which makes a good lookout post.

Gradually, summer softened into autumn. The days were shorter and cooler, and it became harvest time in the forest.

By September the ground squirrels had ended their summer sleep and were busily preparing for winter. They were very active, filling their burrows with food for the cold months ahead.

They gathered acorns and pine nuts and seeds from the brown, green, and golden trees. They climbed up the tree trunks and onto the branches to find the choicest acorns. When the winds blew, many nuts fell to the ground, which made them easier to collect. The squirrels stuffed these treasures into their cheek pouches and scurried back to the dens to deposit the nuts and seeds in their underground storerooms.

The ground squirrel's cheek pouches are like collecting bags. They are openings inside the squirrel's cheeks which, when filled with food, stretch like rubber bands. Each pouch is about an inch long and half an inch high, which

The cheek pouches are like collecting bags.

can expand to a length of around two inches when filled. The animal often takes food directly from the pouches into the mouth, for immediate eating, as well as using the pouches for storage.

The young squirrel found so many nuts for his pouches that he looked as though he had mumps most of the time. In fact, he collected so much food that he had to add a storeroom to his den, which he dug off the main tunnel.

Sometimes he wandered too far from home, into the territories of other kinds of squirrels, where he wasn't welcome. They were also hunting for food and didn't want to share.

One day he galloped along the river, hopping onto rocks and fallen logs, gobbling up seeds and nuts. His pouches were very full when he spied a golden-mantled ground squirrel sitting on a rock. It was small, less than a foot long, and reddish-brown in color, with one white and two black stripes on each side. It quickly turned, peered back at the intruder, and ran for its burrow. Diving into the hole, it immediately stuck out its head to get a better look. When it gave a loud, scolding chirp, the lively young squirrel fled back to his own area.

A golden-mantled ground squirrel peering from its burrow.

Another day he got into a loud argument with a gray squirrel. The gray squirrel lived in the trees and only scurried down to earth to bury nuts and seeds in the ground. These would be his main food supply during the coming winter. He industriously gathered and hid acorns and pine nuts in shallow holes about three inches deep. Sometimes he stopped, sheared off the top of an acorn, and ate the nutmeat. Then he returned to the treetops to collect more.

It was a warm, misty fall morning, and the ground

A gray squirrel perched on a limb.

squirrel roamed farther than usual from his rock and burrow. The fragrant scents of newly fallen acorns lured him deeper and deeper into the forest. As he began to forage, he dug up a fresh ripe nut and then another and another. His boney fingers could hardly stuff them into his mouth fast enough. It was more than he could possibly eat, and his cheek pouches began to bulge. Suddenly, there was a shrieking from the tree branches above him.

The sound was repeated many times and became higher pitched and louder.

The young ground squirrel froze, listening. Then he looked up.

There was the gray squirrel, perched on a limb, barking down at him in outrage. It was as though he were scolding him, saying, "Get away from those nuts. This is my territory, and all nuts are mine!"

When the gray squirrel started to scuttle down the tree trunk, the young ground squirrel let out a long squeak. He raced back through the forest as fast as he could and dived into his safe burrow. Later, in the quiet, he ate the rest of the gray squirrel's acorns from his pouches.

The first storm came in October. By then the young squirrel and all of the other ground squirrels had become very fat. He had eaten as much as he could hold of the rich nuts and seeds, and his burrow storeroom was full.

When the winds began to howl, and the air became cold, he crawled into his burrow and went to sleep. He curled up in a ball, with his nose against his rump, and began to hibernate. Now his body wouldn't require food for awhile. Sometimes he woke up and ate the good nuts from his storeroom and then went back to sleep again. He wasn't even aware of winter's violent storms raging above him.

It wasn't until the beginning of March, with the first stirrings of spring, that he fully awakened. His food supply was low, and he would soon leave the burrow to forage and find a mate.

Now he was ready to lead the life of a grown-up ground squirrel.

INDEX

AUTHOR/PHOTOGRAPHER

Colleen Stanley Bare is a free-lance writer and photographer and has had hundreds of articles and poems published in major national magazines and newspapers. Long interested in photography, many of her travel articles have been illustrated with her photographs.

A native Californian, she is married, has two sons, and holds an A.B. in psychology from Stanford University and an M.A. in educational psychology from the University of California, Berkeley.

She is the author of *The Durable Desert Tortoise*.